Play-Along Songs

Musical Activities for Children

Volume 1

D1408265

Ken and Georgia Frawley

Production Associates, Inc.

Production Associates, Inc.
1206 West Collins Ave.
Orange, CA 92867
www.playalongsongs.com

Printed in the United States of America

Publisher's Cataloging-in-Publication data

Frawley, Ken.
    Play-along songs : music and movement activities, volume 1 / Ken and Georgia Frawley.
    p. cm.
    Series : Play-Along Songs
    ISBN 9781887120050
1. Movement education. 2. Singing games. 3. Games with music. 4. Children's songs. 5. Dance for children.
6. Early childhood education --Activity programs. I. Frawley, Georgia. II. Series. III. Title.

GV452 .F73 2011
372.86/8 --dc22

Executive Project Director: Mike Cash
Cover and Interior Design: Ben Marker and Ken Frawley
Copy Editing: PeopleSpeak
Music editing: Richard Abraham
Models: Sarah Frawley and John Frawley
Photography: Mark Seaton

Songs By (original and adapted)
Ken Frawley: Animal Choir; Cowboys Like to Ride; Going Up the Mountain; If I Had a Fiddle; I'm
    Thinking of an Animal; Jumping; Slowly Walks the Dinosaur; Stop, Look, and Listen; Walking Through
    the Forest; What a Nice Day.
Georgia Frawley and Ken Frawley: Open and Close; Up, Up, Up We Go.
Amanda Carnegie and Ken Frawley: Can You Do?
John Frawley and Ken Frawley: Lions and Tigers

Contents

Alphabetical Listing with Categories

Acknowledgments

I want to thank many people who have influenced my journey. First, thanks go to my wife, Georgia, whose unwavering support and creative thoughts have made all my work possible. Dan Crow's kind words encouraged me to begin performing and start my adventure. Clare Carnegie and Terry Tiritilli have played a major part in my performances and recordings, supporting me in all of my efforts every step of the way. I am grateful to my daughter Coreen, who provides the vocals for many of my songs, and to my daughter, Sarah, and son, John, for years of performing with me and for being the signing models for this book. I want to express my deep appreciation to Richard Abraham for his contributions to the production, arrangement, and recording of the songs. I also want to thank my fellow children's music artists Bob Harrison and Dave Kinnoin for their support in all my endeavors.

Libraries have played a key role in the development of this product line. Librarians throughout Southern California have repeatedly booked my programs. I especially want to thank Ilene Abramson and Maureen Wade with the Los Angeles Public Library who have supported my work from the very beginning. I want to recognize Janine Jacobs with the City of Fullerton Library and Ginger Safstrom with the City of Temecula Library, who have always been wonderful to me, have supported my work, and have always been there to cheer me on.

I want to thank Mike Cash, who not only helped to develop and create the books but also the We Sign DVD series of signing songs and the Sign to Speak books. Finally, I want to recognize Mark Seaton, who helped me understand midi and audio recordings and came to my technological rescue countless times as I developed *Play-Along Songs*.

— Ken Frawley

Music has always been a major part of my life. My thanks go to my parents, my teachers from kindergarten all the way through high school choir, and Girl Scouts for over thirty years of music. My husband and children have been an inspiration for ideas and fun. It is amazing how songs just happen on an eight-hour road trip.

— Georgia Frawley

This book is dedicated to a dear friend and supporter
Jim "Santa" Lewis-Hetrick (1932-2010).
His generous heart, warm smile, selfless spirit,
and insightful thoughts shall be missed.

Introduction

This *Play-Along Songs* book is the result of thousands of interactive musical performances presented to children of all ages. Every song, from traditional to original titles, has been developed and perfected through over 30 years of presentations, musical programs, and concerts given to over one million children and family groups at preschools, libraries, schools, fairs, festivals, scouting events, summer camps, and many other types of city and community events. These songs actively involve children in physical, playful, and imaginative ways that allow them to become part of the musical experience.

Each song in this book was chosen because of its appeal to children. Parents, teachers, camp directors, scout leaders, and caregivers will find that every song contained within this book offers unique, interactive, and playful opportunities to not only have musical fun with their children but also enhance and support learning. The songs in this collection do not require any special singing or musical skills—all that is needed is the desire to have fun by singing, moving, and playing along with children.

Play-Along Songs includes musical activities that encourage children to use their voices, bodies, and minds to have fun and learn. Some songs feature movements ranging from upper-body actions and finger plays to full-body actions that tap into children's energy in a focused way, helping them to develop their fine and gross motor skills. Other songs allow children to create new verses, actions, sounds, and rhymes with their own words and imaginations.

Music in the educational process has been an ageless part of human experience. Howard Gardner has identified at least eight learning styles called "multiple intelligences." He believes that learning through music is a powerful way to learn, but engaging several intelligences within an activity further enhances learning. *Play-Along Songs* does just that by offering children a rich and varied learning experience using many different intelligences all at the same time, including:

- Kinesthetic learning through physical movement
- Visual learning through seeing the actions and signs
- Oral learning through singing and using language
- Interpersonal learning through interacting with others
- Musical learning through singing songs and rhyming

By combining these learning styles into one activity, we create a powerful way for children to remember language and concepts like the ABCs, numbers, colors, and rhymes. Think back to any action songs you learned as a child. Songs like "Itsy Bitsy Spider" and "I'm a Little Teapot" are easily remembered, and the movements are locked into memory.

Within this book you will find familiar songs and rhymes featuring traditional movements, as well as adaptations that will make them even more fun and interesting. Additionally, there are original songs that have proven to provide children with playful and innovative experiences. Also included are songs featuring American Sign Language (ASL), and language manipulation. These participatory musical experiences provide children with a great way to appreciate music and learn about beat, tempo, rhythm, and self-expression.

Play-along songs are easy to learn, adaptable, helpful in developing creativity, and they are enjoyed by all ages. Beginning at birth, babies love to hear their parents singing. It brings them pleasure and comfort. Toddlers and preschoolers love how the songs allow for adult focus and interaction. This attention lets them know that they are cared for and important to those around them. For older children, activity songs offer challenging actions with playful silliness that can be enjoyed not only with adults but also with other children.

Benefits of *Play-Along Songs*

- Strengthens memory and recall
- Develops fine and gross motor skills and enhances hand-eye coordination
- Improves listening and necessitates following directions
- Increases language skills, vocabulary, and word understanding
- Supports reading readiness
- Reinforces the learning of ABCs, colors, numbers, rhymes and more
- Cultivates an appreciation for music
- Fosters self-esteem and self-confidence
- Encourages creativity, adaptability and imagination
- Connects body and mind through thoughtful skills and movements
- Promotes social skills through turn-taking and cooperation
- Engages children and adults in bonding activities

How to Use the Book

This book is designed to provide teachers, parents, and other caregivers with a clear understanding of how to sing and perform each song. The songs feature:

- Melody lines with lyrics and chords
- Informative introductions featuring insights and creative tips
- Pictures to clarify the gestures, movements, and signs
- Online instruction, demonstrations, and support
- iTunes links for song recordings

The songs often contain indicators to help you understand where and how the actions occur. Words that are capitalized (for example, STOP) indicate an ASL sign. Words in parentheses [for example, (clap)] indicate specific action or direction. There are also separate action lines found in the sheet music to help understand the movements.

Most of the songs are supported by pictures to clearly demonstrate the movements and signs that are in the song. Self-explanatory actions (for example, jump, walk, hop, clap) will not have pictures. You may choose as many or as few of the actions, signs, and ideas offered in any song as you like depending on what you are comfortable with and feel you can lead effectively. Be sure to keep all movements and activities age-appropriate. It is also helpful to review each song's introduction. Here you will find tips, advice, experiences, and creative use information that will help you perform the song and encourage creativity.

You do not need to read music, play an instrument, know any sign language, or have any singing or musical talent to use *Play-Along Songs*. All the songs in this book can be performed a cappella, with an instrument, or by singing and moving along to songs downloaded from iTunes. Keep in mind that children place no judgments on vocal or musical skills. If you really find singing to be impossible, chanting is an option. Children derive pleasure from the engaged interaction of adults.

This book features an alphabetical listing and graph that provides you with a quick guide to finding the type of song that best fits your needs and interests. This chart helps you decide on the scope of the action (full body, ASL, etc.) and the type of song (animals, imagination, zipper, etc.) that you would like to use with your children. Once you select a song you can learn it from the sheet music or from the online support.

How to Use *Play-Along Songs* with Children

The following points will help you to choose, learn, adapt, and effectively use the songs in this book.

1. **Guide your children.** By being guided through the songs as they learn the words, melodies, actions, and concepts, children learn about rhyming, language, and using their imaginations in the creative process.

2. **Choose age-appropriate songs.** The songs in this book can be used with babies all the way up through preadolescents. When choosing a song, be sure the actions and vocabulary are age-appropriate for your group. Children respond to and have fun with activities they are capable of accomplishing.

3. **Alter the songs as needed.** Adapt the movements and signs in any of the songs to meet the needs of your children. Here are some suggestions:

   - **For babies.** Short songs with simple actions are best. Young children love to watch and listen to their parents singing and moving. You can enhance babies' involvement by moving their arms, wiggling their legs, bouncing them on your knee, or helping them to imitate the movement in the song.

   - **For toddlers.** Simple and repetitive songs with actions and a few signs are ideal to use with this group. This allows toddlers to participate in each song and feel successful. It is also an excellent age to begin having children choose their own activities, animals, sounds, and actions.

   - **For older children.** Preschool and elementary ages like not only to be challenged but also to be silly and have fun. Choose playful songs that have complicated actions, feature sign language, and will stimulate children's creativity by having them make up their own verses, lyrics, and rhymes.

4. **Read first.** Read the information section before each song as it often provides directions, information, tips, and insights that are specific to that song.

5. **Learn the songs.** Learn each song as it is written—how to sing it and perform the actions—and understand any related creative concepts before introducing it.

6. **Have your children's attention.** Begin the song when children are paying attention and are ready to join you.

7. **Follow your children's lead.** Though you will often lead the *Play-Along Songs* activities, be sure to watch your children and take cues from them. What would they like to do? Do they want to continue or move on to another song? What do they want to say or sing about? The songs can often be rewritten to reflect their ideas. What actions do they want to use? Move in the direction and manner in which the children want to perform the actions. Being in tune with your children allows you to be both guide and follower at the same time.

8. **Explain and teach the movements.** Simple explanations for familiar actions are fine, but you will need to demonstrate signs and movements that children do not easily understand. Teach actions slowly, with children repeating them after you.

9. **Talk, chant, or sing the songs a cappella.** It is often effective to say or sing the words without an instrument when introducing and performing songs. This helps you begin a song slowly and speed up the tempo as your children's ability increases.

10. **Lead the songs at tempo.** Once a song is learned, sing and play along at the normal speed of the song. When the children know the actions of a song, it is easy to lead it using an instrument or the related music which is available on iTunes. Visit playalongsongs.com for links.

11. **Lead all the songs with enthusiasm.** Use exaggerated facial expressions, voice, and movements. Children appreciate your zeal.

12. **Keep the song activities fun and playful.** Try to make sure that children really enjoy these activities and never find them tedious or, worse still, coercive.

13. **Praise and reward all efforts.** Support and encourage all your children's efforts, helping them to strive for and succeed in mastering each song's movements and concepts.

14. **Repeat the songs often.** Children love repetition and often will want to repeat songs over and over.

15. **Create a special time for using *Play-Along Songs*.** Having a special time every day for singing and playing songs helps children develop an enthusiasm for participating in these activities. Singing in the car makes trips go faster and keeps everyone involved.

Playing an Instrument with These Songs

Here are a few ways to effectively perform these songs with an instrument:

- Choose a song that has clear and easy-to-understand actions (for example, jump, wiggle, clap, roar) requiring no demonstration.

- Teach and practice the movements with the children before starting the song. For more complicated songs, begin with a few actions and add more as the children become familiar with the song.

- Choose one child or a group of children to stand in front of the others to lead the movements of the song while you play an instrument.

- When a song and its actions become familiar, it is easy to play an instrument while the children perform the actions on their own.

Creativity with Songs

Over the years, folk songs and rhymes have been adapted and changed to create new songs. It's not difficult to understand why. Folk songs are easy to sing and have memorable melodies, simple words, and often a repetitive chorus. In the introductory section to each song, you will find suggestions on how to adapt that song and lead children through the creative process of developing actions, choosing different animals or things, and writing new words and rhymes. Adapting songs is a terrific way for children to learn how to use and manipulate language. Once you have learned a song and are confident in performing it with children, you can begin to lead them in the creative process of changing words, rhymes, actions, and sounds.

Action songs are easily adaptable. Children can change the order in which actions are performed and even choose new ones to use in the song. Keep in mind that you can control the level of activity by explaining to your children that the actions they choose must be able to be performed sitting down or just using their hands and arms – or, if space permits, any action they would like to do.

Songs featuring animal sounds are also easy to change. Children can choose to alter the order of the animals, or they can choose to sing and make the sounds or movements of new animals. Usually, children choose common animals and well-known sounds, but sometimes they pick some pretty funny animals. I have had children pick flatworms, naked mole rats, and even starfish. In cases such as these, ask the children to come up with a sound or an action. Don't worry about whether the sound has any connection to reality—just follow their imaginative lead.

Rhyming requires a little more work. You can begin with a demonstration of how rhyming works. Explain how words like "hat" and "cat" or "car" and "star" rhyme. Then encourage your children to come up with rhymes for other words. You'll find yourself amazed at the words and ideas children can come up with.

When you encourage children to alter words, choose actions, use their language skills, and stretch their imaginations, you not only get them involved, but you also help them develop a sense of accomplishment and the self-confidence that comes from creating something new and fun. In keeping with the purposes of this book (to encourage creativity and playfully engage children with music), please adapt the songs to meet your and your children's interests.

American Sign Language with Songs

Signing is a great way to add movement to songs. ASL's letters and words are signed through hand and arm movements along with facial expressions. ASL is one of the most common languages in the United States, and children find it to be both fun and challenging. Signs found in the songs can be used during regular conversation and with other activities throughout the day. Many signed songs in *Play-Along Songs* books are from the We Sign DVD series. We will list, in song introductions, the We Sign DVD title on which a song can be found. For more information on signing with songs, visit www.wesign.com or www.signtospeak.com.

SING/SONG
(Swing hand
across forearm)

SIGN
(Move hands in a
circle toward chest)

Online Support

We believe that music books often do not provide enough information and support so that parents, teachers, and caregivers can understand how to present, sing, and perform the participatory songs they present. To make our songs easier to understand, *Play-Along Songs* offers instructions, tips, melody lines with guitar chords, and clear pictures demonstrating song movements. In addition, our online support will provide everyone, even those with no musical background, more assistance and understanding on using our songs with children.

Play-Along Songs online support is accessed by visiting www.playalongsongs.com and entering this code: PAS101A. Here are some of the beneficial materials you will find on the website.

- Instructional videos that:
    - Demonstrate the movements.
    - Provide additional presentation insights and tips.
    - Offer expanded how-to information.
    - Discuss songs and how to encourage children to creatively adapt them.
- Recordings of the songs that can be listened to online.
- Links to iTunes so that you can download the songs from this book for your own CD collection.

Play-Along Songs combines books with recordings and online instructional support so that everyone will be successful at using these songs with children and benefit from our years of musical experience with children.

Play-Along Songs
Volume 1

Jumping

Get ready to move all around to this very energetic song that children really enjoy. Use the actions found in the song, or pick your own. There are also two ASL signs in this song. These words are capitalized. First is the sign for STOP, which is a very fun and effective way to STOP the action. Second is the sign for SO CAN I, and it is used at the end of each verse. For movements like marching or walking, have the children move in a circle. You can also rework the actions in this song so it can be performed while sitting. For instance, instead of the children skipping or jumping, have them snap their fingers or clap their hands. Find the signed version of this song on We Sign *Playtime*.

STOP - 1   **STOP - 2**

SO CAN I
("Y" hand move in & out)

Jumping

Words and Music by
Ken Frawley

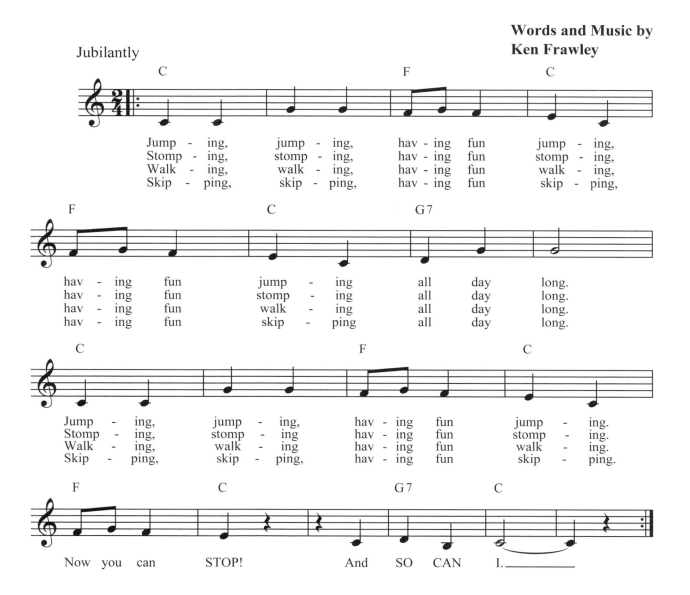

5. Wiggling, wiggling, having fun wiggling,
   Having fun wiggling all day long.
   Wiggling, wiggling, having fun wiggling.
   Now you can STOP - and SO CAN I.

Other Suggestions

Laughing	Flying
Clapping	Marching
Hopping	Dancing
Twirling	Whispering

American Sign Language Alphabet

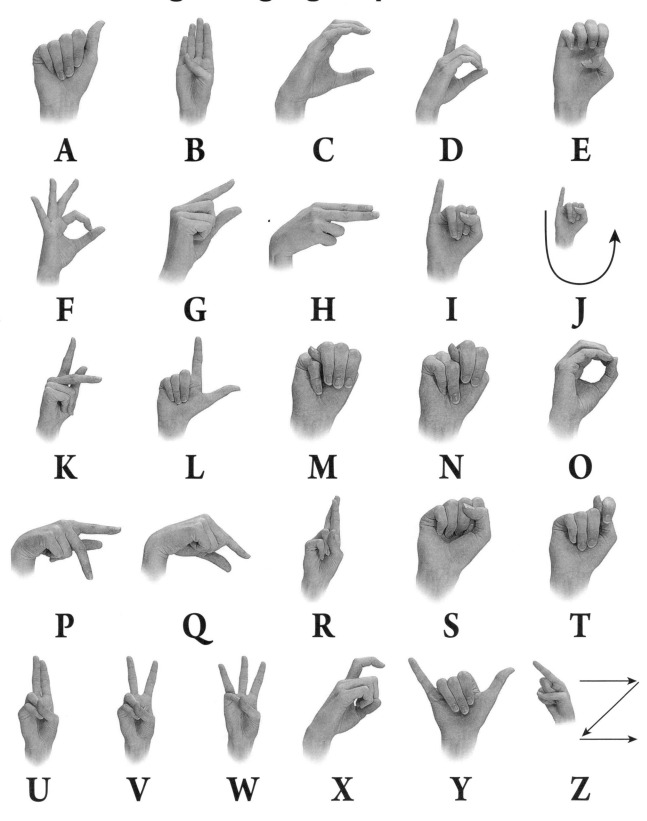

ABC Sign Song

Learning the ABCs with sign language is a great way for children to memorize and remember their letters. A real benefit to signing this song is that it provides for clear letter separation. Children often think that L-M-N-O-P is just one letter, but signing allows them to see, make, and say each letter individually. It is best to learn the signs first and then teach and demonstrate them before singing and signing the song. When signing the letters, use your dominate hand held up near your shoulder. Begin slowly and pick up speed as the children's competency increases. Once children are comfortable, you might even try singing and signing the alphabet backwards. You will find that signed words are capitalized. Find this song on We Sign *ABC*.

HAPPY

SIGN

Little Cabin in the Woods

Here is a great camp song sung in two segments that is full of actions. The first segment has everyone singing the song while making the movements for the specific words pictured below. Start out slowly and pick up the tempo until the children sing and move as fast as they can. In the second segment of the song, follow the "Action" line in the sheet music and perform the actions *without* singing the words. Again, start out slowly and increase the speed with each round.

Cabin - 1   **Cabin - 2**   **Woods**

Window   **Saw**   **Rabbit**
(Rabbit hopping)   **Knock**
(Like knocking)

Help Me - 1   **Help Me - 2**   **Hunter**

Little Cabin in the Woods

Traditional

Slowly, then repeated with increasing tempo

Dead **Dread** **Come** **Hide**

Head and Shoulders

This children's song about body parts is a traditional favorite. As you sing the song, point to or touch the corresponding body parts. Start out singing and moving slowly to establish the melody and the order of the body parts. Gradually speed up the tempo until you are singing and moving as fast as you can. You can also adapt the song to feature other body parts. Movements are self-explanatory.

22

A Sailor Went to Sea

This camp song favorite features a variety of silly movements. Each verse is first sung with its own action. Then the final verse has the children combine all the actions into one long verse. Sing this last verse slowly the first time through, then increase the tempo each time you repeat it until you are singing and moving as fast as you can. Make the movements as you sing the words.

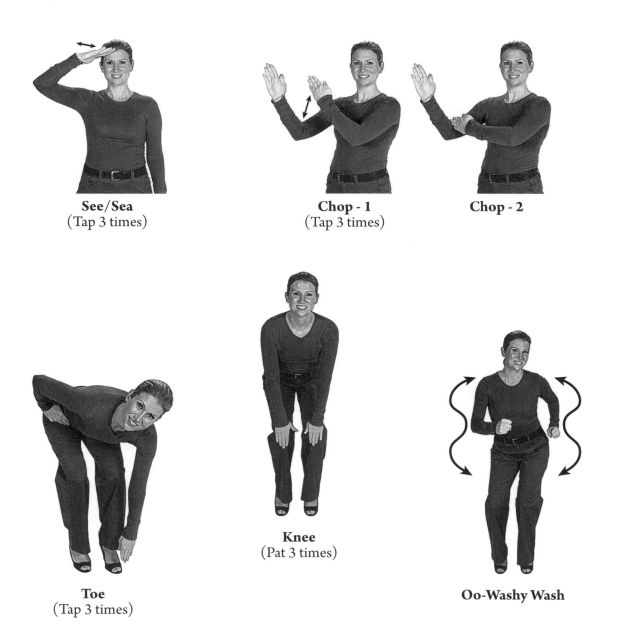

See/Sea
(Tap 3 times)

Chop - 1
(Tap 3 times)

Chop - 2

Toe
(Tap 3 times)

Knee
(Pat 3 times)

Oo-Washy Wash

A Sailor Went to Sea

Traditional

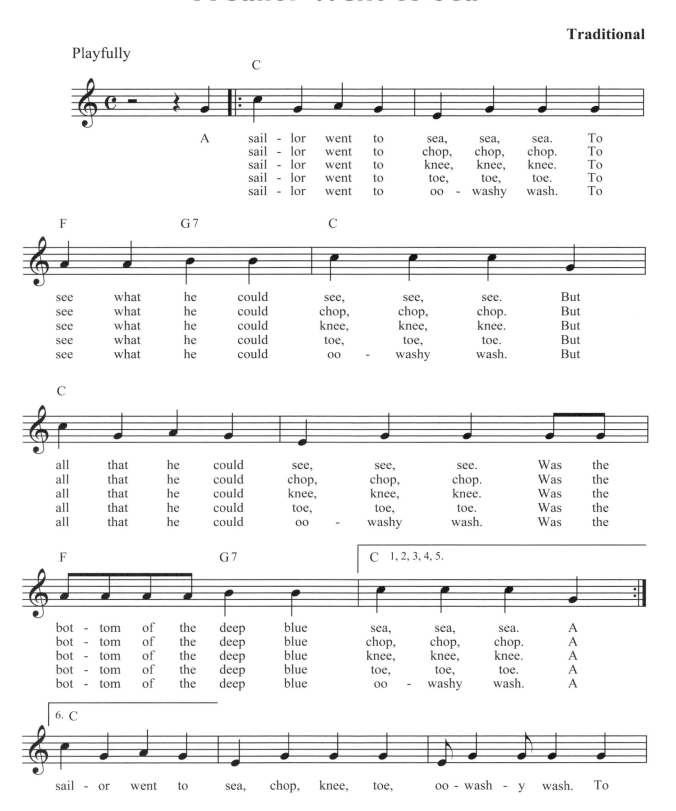

A Sailor Went to Sea

see what he could see, chop, knee, toe, oo - wash - y wash. But

all that he could see, chop, knee, toe, oo - wash - y wash. Was the

bot - tom of the deep blue sea, chop, knee, toe, oo - wash - y wash.

Open and Close

Learning about opposites is fun and physical in this song. Discussing and demonstrating the meaning of opposites such as up/down and big/small before you start is helpful. Then show the children the action for each of the opposites that will be sung. If you have a group of children, choose a few to lead the actions as you play the song on a guitar, piano, or other instrument.

| Open | Close | Up | Down |

| Right | Left | Forward | Back |

| Big | Small | Happy | Sad |

Open and Close

Words and Music by
Ken and Georgia Frawley

5. Big and small. Big and small.
   We all know how to big and small.
   Big and small. Big and small.
   We all know how to big and small.
   We all know how to big and small.

6. Happy and sad. Happy and sad.
   We all know how to happy and sad.
   Happy and sad. Happy and sad.
   We all know how to happy and sad.
   We all know how to happy and sad.

Bingo

This is a spelling song that is performed by replacing each sung letter of "Bingo" with a clap. The song is repeated until all the letters of Bingo are only clapped. Our version has added American Sign Language, ASL, along with singing each letter for B-I-N-G-O. Each verse will have one additional letter remain silent. The final verse has everyone singing and signing along. There are also fun signs for FARMER, DOG, and BINGO. The name sign for Bingo is signed with a letter B held across the body and by the shoulder. Letters are signed with your dominant hand held up by the shoulder. The signed words in the song are capitalized. Find this song on We Sign *Classroom Favorites*.

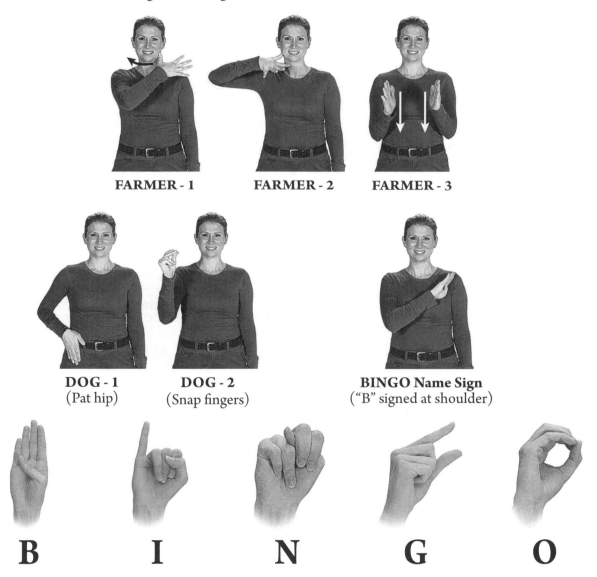

FARMER - 1　　**FARMER - 2**　　**FARMER - 3**

DOG - 1
(Pat hip)

DOG - 2
(Snap fingers)

BINGO Name Sign
("B" signed at shoulder)

B　　**I**　　**N**　　**G**　　**O**

Bingo

Traditional

Cheerfully

There was a FARM - ER had a DOG and

BING - O was his name O!

1. B	I	N	G	O
2. CLAP	I	N	G	O
3. CLAP	CLAP	N	G	O
4. CLAP	CLAP	CLAP	G	O
5. CLAP	CLAP	CLAP	CLAP	O
6. CLAP	CLAP	CLAP	CLAP	CLAP
Sign 7. B	I	N	G	O

B	I	N	G	O
CLAP	I	N	G	O
CLAP	CLAP	N	G	O
CLAP	CLAP	CLAP	G	O
CLAP	CLAP	CLAP	CLAP	O
CLAP	CLAP	CLAP	CLAP	CLAP
B	I	N	G	O

B	I	N	G	O	and
CLAP	I	N	G	O	and
CLAP	CLAP	N	G	O	and
CLAP	CLAP	CLAP	G	O	and
CLAP	CLAP	CLAP	CLAP	O	and
CLAP	CLAP	CLAP	CLAP	CLAP	and
B	I	N	G	O	and

BING - O was his name O!

29

Twinkle, Twinkle Little Star

This is one of the most famous of all Mother Goose nursery rhymes. Young children love to participate in the simple movements of this song. For very young children, use only the movements for "twinkle" while you sing the song.

Twinkle, Twinkle Little Star
(Open and close hands, repeatedly)

Wonder

You Are

**Up Above the
World So High**

Like a Diamond in the Sky

Twinkle, Twinkle Little Star

Traditional

Old Brass Wagon

"Old Brass Wagon" is a classic American square-dance song that has been enjoyed by children and adults alike for generations. This version offers children an opportunity to walk in specific directions, turn around, and march. Once you have learned the song, you can adapt the actions—step to the center and take one step back, bow to the left or right, and stomp your left or right foot.

Traditional

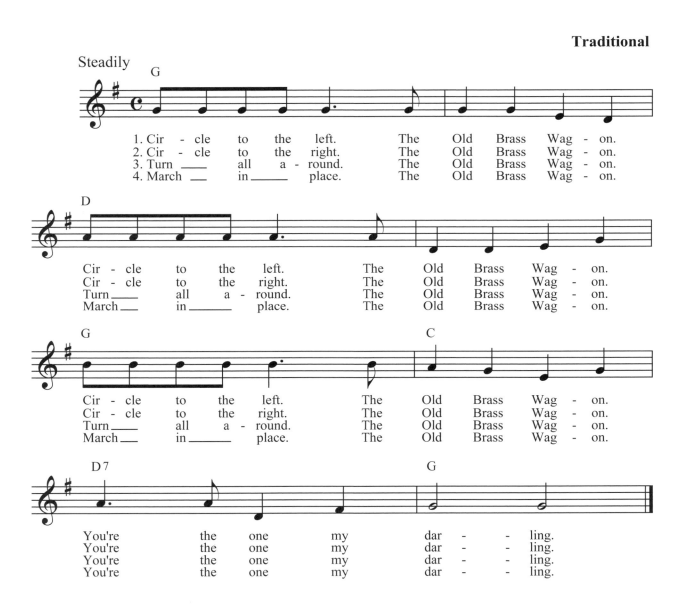

I Had Me a Rooster

This is an old folk song that gets longer and longer with each added animal and sound. Once the song is learned, encourage the children to choose other animals to sing about. If a child chooses an animal that does not make a sound or is unfamiliar, ask the children for help, and they will always provide the solution. I once had a child choose a flatworm, so I asked, "What sound does a flatworm make?" The children quickly informed me that it goes, "Wiggle, wiggle, wiggle." The creative solution worked, and everyone enjoyed singing about a flatworm. You can also sign the animals in this song. Signed words are capitalized.

ROOSTER   CAT - 1   CAT - 2

DUCK - 1   DUCK - 2   COW - 1   COW - 2

LION - 1   LION - 2   TREE
(Twist at wrist)

I Had Me a Rooster

Traditional

I Had Me a Rooster

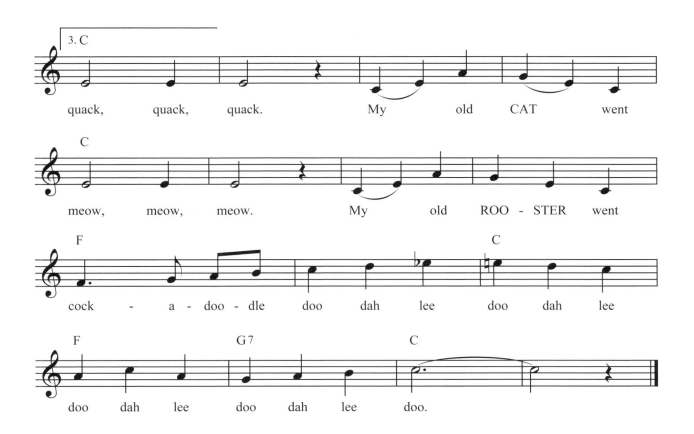

quack,   quack,   quack.   My   old   CAT   went

meow,   meow,   meow.   My   old   ROO - STER   went

cock - a - doo - dle   doo   dah   lee   doo   dah   lee

doo   dah   lee   doo   dah   lee   doo.

4. I had me a COW and the COW pleased me.
   I fed my old COW under yonder TREE.
   My old COW went moo…..
   My old DUCK went quack, quack, quack, quack.
   My old CAT went meow, meow, meow.
   My old ROOSTER went cock-a-doodle doo dah lee,
   Doo da lee, doo dah lee, doo dah lee doo.

5. I had me a LION and the LION pleased me.
   I fed my old LION very carefully.
   My old LION went roar.
   My old COW went moo…..
   My old DUCK went quack, quack, quack, quack.
   My old CAT went meow, meow, meow.
   My old ROOSTER went cock-a-doodle doo dah lee,
   Doo da lee, doo dah lee, doo dah lee doo.

I'm Thinking of an Animal

Everyone loves to play this game of singing clues to describe animals. The structure is simple. The song has an opening section that is sung before each animal's description: "I'm thinking of an animal. I'll describe it to you. See if you can guess it with a hint or two." In the next section you sing lines of description, one clue at a time (up to four lines of description), pausing for a child to make one guess about the animal before continuing. Once a child guesses the animal, you then sing the line, "That's how I describe a (name of the animal)." With larger groups ask children to raise their hands to be chosen one at a time to keep the activity from getting chaotic.

Demonstrating first by singing and describing three or four animals works best. After that, invite children to come up and describe an animal one clue at a time. You will sing the description of the animal and choose other children to guess what it is. However, if after four or five clues it still has not been discovered, have the child tell everyone the name of the animal they were describing. Then sing the final line of the verse with their animal in the line.

When I have children describe animals, I never know what they are going to choose ahead of time. I guess along with the children. Having a few questions to prompt descriptions is helpful. For example, "What color is it?" or "Is it big or small?" or "Where does it live?" or "What sound does it make?" Sometimes children will offer descriptions for animals like, "a five-legged purple elephant" or "a one-legged orange cat." Whatever the children describe, support their efforts and sing about the animal. The signed version of this song can be found on We Sign *More Animals*.

I'm Thinking of an Animal

**Words and Music by
Ken Frawley**

Chorus
3. It has four legs (pause for a guess).
   It has a long tail (pause for a guess).
   It has very sharp teeth (pause for a guess).
   It likes to eat Captain Hook - a crocodile
   That's how I describe a crocodile.

Chorus
4. It has six legs (pause for a guess).
   And it's very, very small (pause for a guess).
   It's black (pause for a guess).
   And it lives on dogs - a flea.
   That's how I describe a flea.

Going Up the Mountain

Everyone gets to use their imaginations and pretend to be walking, with their hands, up a mountain. This song features the ASL numbers for 1 through 5. March up the mountain both left and right to the rhythm of the music.

Position 1

Position 2

Position 3

Position 4

Position 5

Position 6

1 By 1

2 By 2

3 By 3

4 By 4

5 By 5

Going Up the Mountain

Words and Music by
Ken Frawley

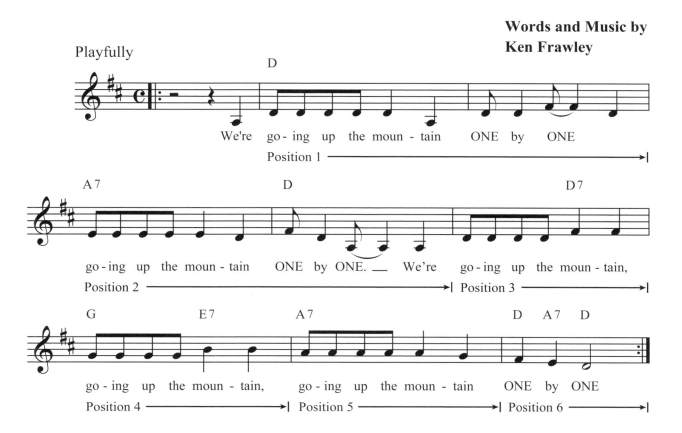

Playfully

We're go-ing up the moun-tain ONE by ONE

Position 1

go-ing up the moun-tain ONE by ONE. __ We're go-ing up the moun-tain,

Position 2 ——————► Position 3 ——————►

go-ing up the moun-tain, go-ing up the moun-tain ONE by ONE

Position 4 ——————► Position 5 ——————► Position 6 ——————►

2. We're going up the mountain TWO by TWO.
   We're going up the mountain TWO by TWO.
   We're going up the mountain,
   Going up the mountain,
   Going up the mountain TWO by TWO.

3. We're going up the mountain THREE by THREE.
   We're going up the mountain THREE by THREE.
   We're going up the mountain,
   Going up the mountain,
   Going up the mountain THREE by THREE.

4. We're going up the mountain FOUR by FOUR.
   We're going up the mountain FOUR by FOUR.
   We're going up the mountain,
   Going up the mountain,
   Going up the mountain FOUR by FOUR.

5. We're going up the mountain FIVE by FIVE.
   We're going up the mountain FIVE by FIVE.
   We're going up the mountain,
   Going up the mountain,
   Going up the mountain FIVE by FIVE.

I'm a Little Piece of Tin

This is a song about a car that has been a campfire favorite for years. It has silly and simple motions that are sung and performed slowly at first, then sped up verse by verse until the song is sung as fast as possible. The fun really starts when ending the song. Everyone needs to end on "Honk, honk!" However, if someone accidently continues to sing "Rattle, rattle…" then everyone has to sing the song over again. This continues until everyone ends on "Honk, honk!"

I	Little	Piece of Tin
Nobody Knows	Shape	Four Wheels
Running Board	I'm Not	Honk (Pull Ear)

I'm a Little Piece of Tin

Traditional

Slowly, then repeated with increasing tempo

I'm a lit - tle piece of tin. No - bo - dy knows what shape I'm in.

Got four wheels and a run - ning board. I'm not a Che - vy and

I'm not a Ford. Honk, honk, rat - tle, rat - tle, rat - tle, crash, beep, beep. Honk,

honk, rat - tle, rat - tle, rat - tle, crash, beep, beep. Honk, honk.

Rattle

Crash

Beep
(Tap twice)

Where Is Thumbkin?

This classic children's finger play song is to the same melody as "Frere Jacques" or "Are You Sleeping." The song begins with your hands and fingers behind your back. They then come out one hand at a time to face each other. Each finger is extended and bent at the knuckle as they sing to each other. Look at your fingers when they are singing to each other as it focuses everyone's attention to the movement. Finally, fingers will "run away" and move back behind your back. Look at the picture of the hand for the names of each finger.

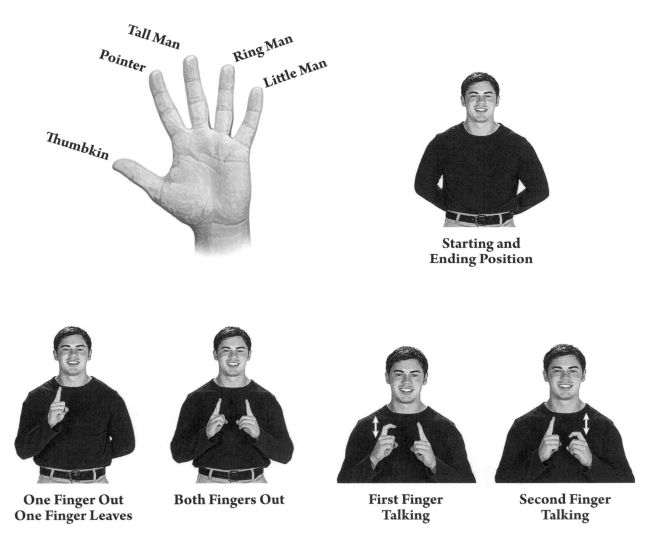

Starting and Ending Position

**One Finger Out
One Finger Leaves**

Both Fingers Out

First Finger Talking

Second Finger Talking

Where Is Thumbkin?

Traditional

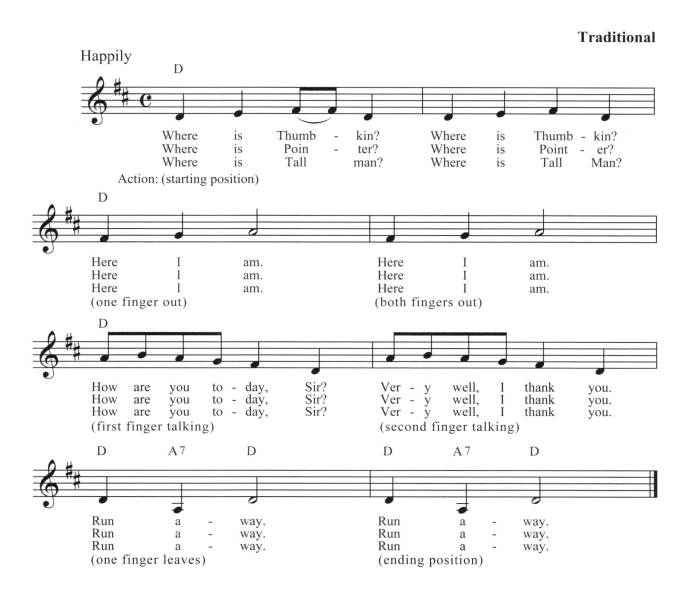

Happily

D

Where is Thumb - kin? Where is Thumb - kin?
Where is Poin - ter? Where is Point - er?
Where is Tall man? Where is Tall Man?

Action: (starting position)

D

Here I am. Here I am.
Here I am. Here I am.
Here I am. Here I am.
(one finger out) (both fingers out)

D

How are you to - day, Sir? Ver - y well, I thank you.
How are you to - day, Sir? Ver - y well, I thank you.
How are you to - day, Sir? Ver - y well, I thank you.
(first finger talking) (second finger talking)

D   **A7**   **D**   **D**   **A7**   **D**

Run a - way. Run a - way.
Run a - way. Run a - way.
Run a - way. Run a - way.
(one finger leaves) (ending position)

4. Where is Ring Man?
Where is Ring Man?
Here I am. Here I am.
How are you today Sir?
Very well, I thank you.
Run away. Run away.

5. Where is Little Man?
Where is Little Man?
Here I am. Here I am.
How are you today Sir?
Very well, I thank you.
Run away. Run away.

6. Where are all the men?
Where are all the men?
Here we are. Here we are.
How are you today Sirs?
Very well, we thank you.
Run away. Run away.

I'm a Little Teapot

Let's pretend to be teapots. Start by describing what a teapot is and how it works. Explain that when the water boils, teapots will make a whistling sound. This means the water is ready to make tea. You then will take a teapot, tip it over, and pour the water out. Included here are new verses that continue the movements and fun as you sing-along and play-along. This adaptation is another example of how to expand upon a traditional song.

Standing Short and Stout

Handle on Left

Handle on Right

Spout On Left

Spout On Right

Tip Over Left

Tip Over Right

Two Handles

Two Spouts

I'm a Little Teapot

**Traditional
New Words by
Ken Frawley**

Rhythmically

I'm a lit - tle tea - pot short and stout.
I'm a lit - tle tea - pot. Yes, it's true.
Now I have two spouts! Pour left and right.

Here is my han - dle, here is my spout.
There's some - thing more that I can ___ do.
Now I have two han - dles. Hold on ___ tight.

When I get all steamed up hear me shout!
I can change my han - dle and my spout!
Now I have one han - dle and one spout!

Tip me o - ver and pour me out.
Tip me o - ver and pour me out.
Tip me o - ver and pour me out.

One, Two, Buckle My Shoe

Learning to count to ten has been taught for years with this Mother Goose nursery rhyme. Children love the challenge of adding the signs for the numbers 1 through 10 and other words as they sing. You will find the signed words capitalized. This song is especially fun when the tempo is increased with each repetition until the song is sung and signed as fast as possible. Numbers are signed with your dominant hand held up near your shoulder. Find this song on We Sign *Numbers*.

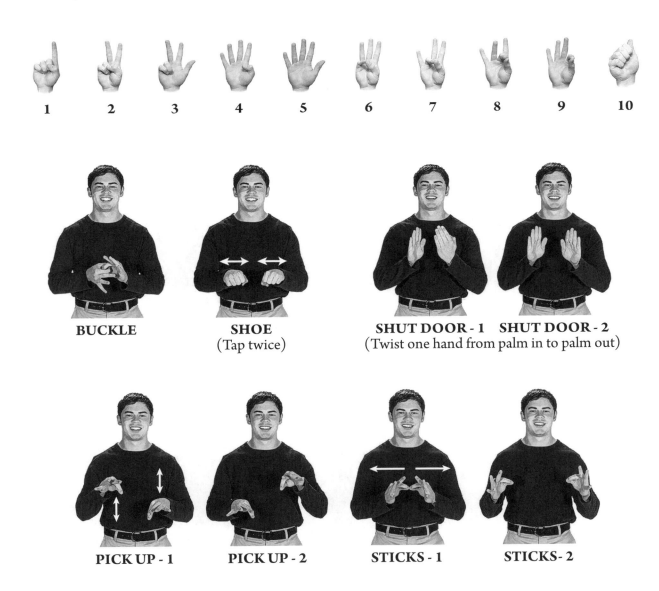

1   2   3   4   5   6   7   8   9   10

BUCKLE   **SHOE**
(Tap twice)

SHUT DOOR - 1   SHUT DOOR - 2
(Twist one hand from palm in to palm out)

PICK UP - 1   **PICK UP - 2**   **STICKS - 1**   **STICKS- 2**

One, Two, Buckle My Shoe

Traditional

Slowly, then repeated with increasing tempo

ONE, TWO BUCK - LE my SHOE. THREE, FOUR

SHUT THE DOOR.___ FIVE, SIX PICK UP STICKS.___ SEV - EN, EIGHT

LAY THEM STRAIGHT. NINE, TEN a BIG red HEN.___

LAY THEM (Moving right to left)

STRAIGHT - 1 **STRAIGHT - 2**

BIG

HEN - 1 **HEN - 2**
(Like the beak of a hen)

Slowly Walks the Dinosaur

Improvisation is a key part to this song. Children love to walk big and mean while stomping their feet, pretending to be dinosaurs. For elephants, they generally walk bent over, with their arms swinging side-to-side like trunks. Arms and hands are flapped for eagles flying, and for snakes I have children wiggle (slither), standing or sitting with their palms together at their chests. Once the song is learned, it is easy for children to be creative. First they choose any animal they wish to sing about, then they choose that animal's movement and sound. I have found that children will choose difficult animals at times. For example, what do you do with a starfish? Have the children decide. In my case they chose to hold their arms open wide with their fingers spread, and the sound was "Blurp, blurp."

**Words and Music by
Ken Frawley**

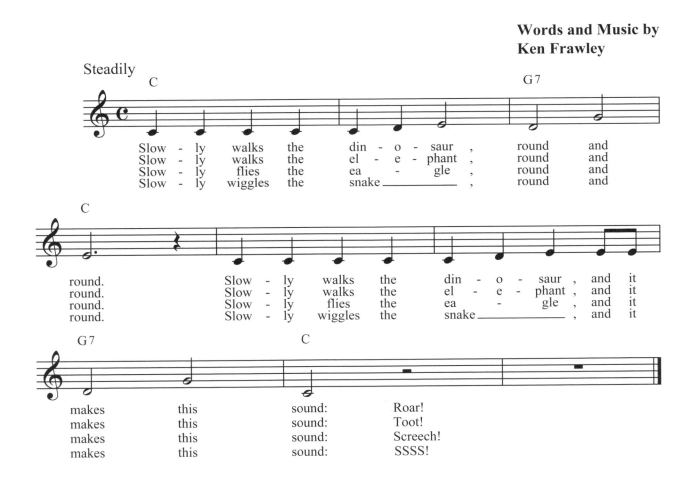

What a Nice Day It Is

This is a fun song that allows children to make up verses about things they like to do on a nice day. Sing the verses to the song as they are here, then invite children to tell you things that can then be sung in the song. "Play with my friends, go to school, play a game" are easy to fit into the song. However, making their descriptions long and fitting them into the song can really add to the fun. For example, you could sing, "It's a nice day to go outside and play baseball with my friend Ryan." Just sing the extended section on the same note quickly.

Words and Music by
Ken Frawley

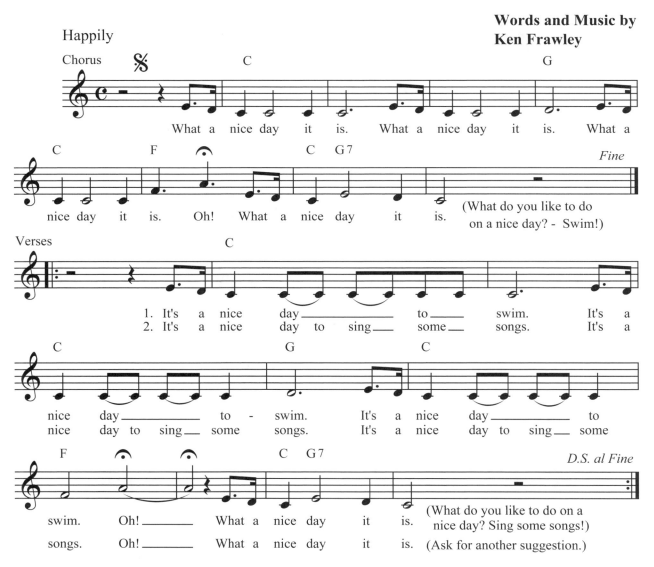

3. It's a nice day to ride my bike.
4. It's a nice day to go to the park and play.

Lions and Tigers

The words to this song are sung to the melody of the song "Head and Shoulders" and feature ASL signs for animals. Start out by teaching the signs with the melody slowly. Repeat for proficiency, and then speed up the tempo of each verse until you sing and move as quickly as you can.

LION - 1   LION - 2   TIGER

BIRD - 1   BIRD - 2   ELEPHANT - 1   ELEPHANT - 2
(Like the beak of a bird)

CAT - 1   CAT - 2   DOG - 1   DOG - 2
                                              (Pat hip)   (Snap fingers)

Lions and Tigers

Music Traditional
New Lyrics by
Ken and John Frawley

Slowly, then repeated with increasing tempo

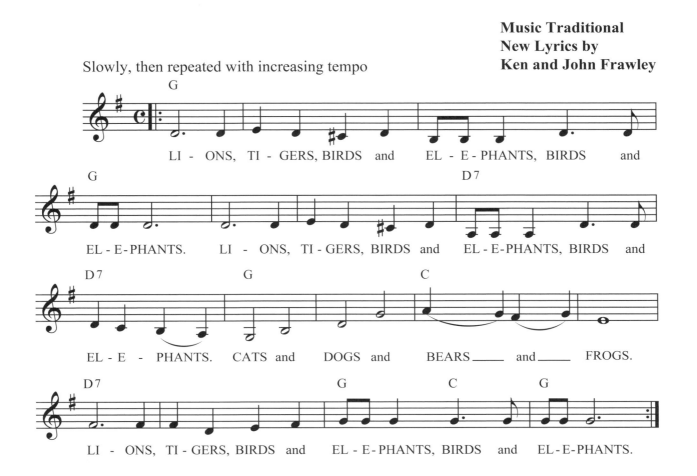

LI - ONS, TI - GERS, BIRDS and EL - E - PHANTS, BIRDS and EL - E - PHANTS. LI - ONS, TI - GERS, BIRDS and EL - E - PHANTS, BIRDS and EL - E - PHANTS. CATS and DOGS and BEARS____ and ____ FROGS. LI - ONS, TI - GERS, BIRDS and EL - E - PHANTS, BIRDS and EL - E - PHANTS.

BEAR - 1   BEAR - 2   FROG - 1   FROG - 2
(Like the legs of a frog)

Itsy Bitsy Spider

This ageless Mother Goose rhyme is also a classic children's finger play. It has been performed and sung for generations. Its movements are simple but can be challenging for very young children.

——— **The Itsy Bitsy Spider Went Up the Water Spout** ———

Down Came Rain - 1
(Wiggle fingers)   **Down Came Rain - 2**   ——— **Washed the Spider Out** ———

Up came the sun   **Dried Up Rain - 1**
(Wiggle fingers)   **Dried Up Rain - 2**

Itsy Bitsy Spider

Traditional

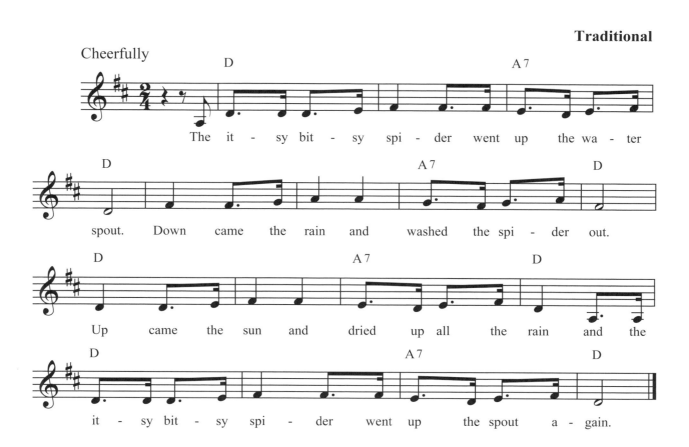

Cheerfully

The it - sy bit - sy spi - der went up the wa - ter

spout. Down came the rain and washed the spi - der out.

Up came the sun and dried up all the rain and the

it - sy bit - sy spi - der went up the spout a - gain.

This Old Man

Here is a traditional song that has been a favorite for generations. It features silly words and actions. Knocking is the action for knick-knack. This version has added the ASL signs for old and the numbers 1 to 10.

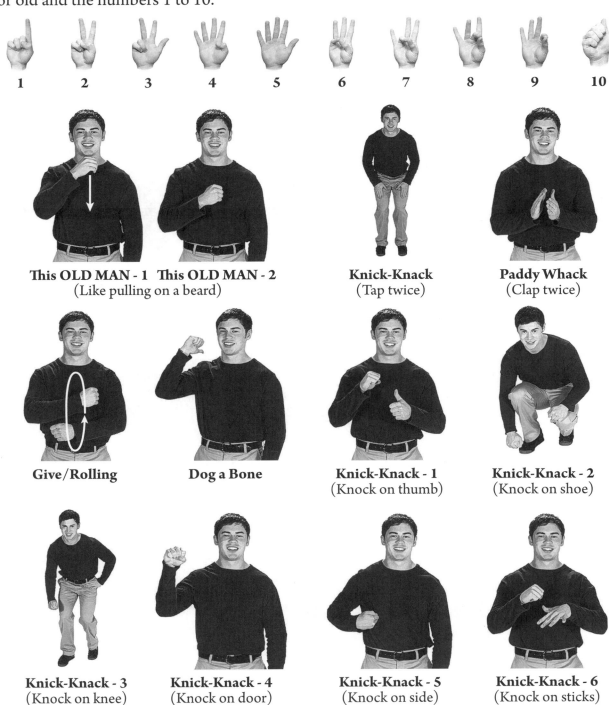

1   2   3   4   5   6   7   8   9   10

This OLD MAN - 1
(Like pulling on a beard)

This OLD MAN - 2

Knick-Knack
(Tap twice)

Paddy Whack
(Clap twice)

Give/Rolling

Dog a Bone

Knick-Knack - 1
(Knock on thumb)

Knick-Knack - 2
(Knock on shoe)

Knick-Knack - 3
(Knock on knee)

Knick-Knack - 4
(Knock on door)

Knick-Knack - 5
(Knock on side)

Knick-Knack - 6
(Knock on sticks)

This Old Man

Traditional

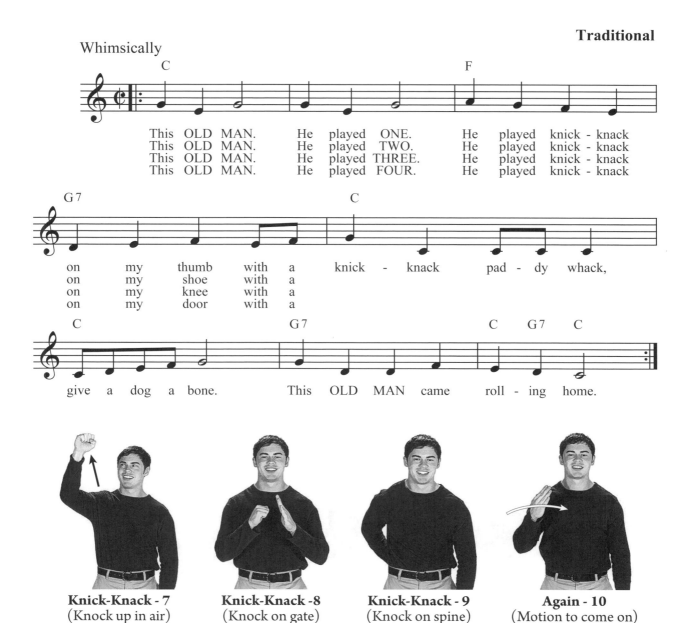

Whimsically

C   F

This OLD MAN. He played ONE. He played knick - knack
This OLD MAN. He played TWO. He played knick - knack
This OLD MAN. He played THREE. He played knick - knack
This OLD MAN. He played FOUR. He played knick - knack

G 7   C

on   my   thumb   with   a   knick - knack   pad - dy   whack,
on   my   shoe   with   a
on   my   knee   with   a
on   my   door   with   a

C   G 7   C   G 7   C

give   a   dog   a   bone.   This   OLD   MAN   came   roll - ing   home.

Knick-Knack - 7
(Knock up in air)

Knick-Knack -8
(Knock on gate)

Knick-Knack - 9
(Knock on spine)

Again - 10
(Motion to come on)

5. This OLD MAN. He played FIVE.
   He played knick-knack on my on my side.
6. This OLD MAN. He played SIX.
   He played knick-knack on my sticks.
7. This OLD MAN. He played SEVEN.
   He played knick-knack up in heaven.

8. This OLD MAN. He played EIGHT.
   He played knick-knack on my gate.
9. This OLD MAN. He played NINE.
   He played knick-knack on my spine.
10. This OLD MAN. He played TEN.
    He played knick-knack once again.

Yankee Doodle

This great American patriotic song becomes even more enjoyable when American Sign Language is added. Reduce the number of signs you use for younger children, and include all of the signs for older ones. Notice that we sign DANCE for the word STEP because in this song that is what it means. The signed words are capitalized. Find this song on We Sign *Patriotic Songs*.

YANKEE
(The letter "Y")

DOODLE
(The letter "D")

RIDING
(Fingers straddling
hand like riding)

PONY
(Bend fingers down)

FEATHER/MACARONI
(Shake hand)

CAP

KEEP IT UP

DANDY
(Wiggle fingers)

MUSIC/SONG

STEP/DANCE

GIRLS

Yankee Doodle

Traditional

In marching time

YAN - KEE DOO - DLE   went to town a - RID-ING   on   a   PO - NY.

Stuck   a   FEA-THER   in   his   CAP   and   called   it   MAC - A - RO - NI.

YAN - KEE DOO - DLE   KEEP IT UP.   YAN - KEE DOO - DLE   DAN - DY.

Mind   the MU - SIC   and   the   STEP, and   with   the   GIRLS   be   han - dy.

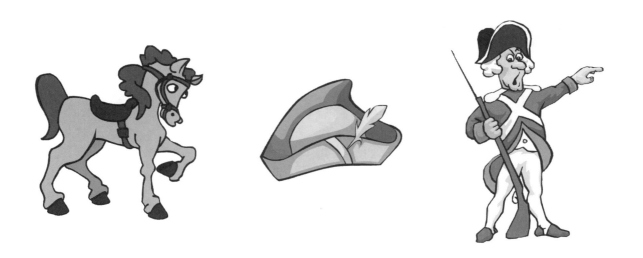

Cowboys Like to Ride

For over one hundred years, cowboys have captured the imaginations of children. This song features movements children can pantomime and sounds they can mimic that all reflect something about cowboys—their work, their life, and the animals that surrounded them. Once you have learned the song, you can add other actions, animals, and sounds.

Ride Horse
(Bounce up and down)

Spin Rope

Cow

Wolves Howl

Yee-haw - 1

Yee-haw - 2

Sleep

Cowboys Like to Ride

**Words and Music by
Ken Frawley**

3. Cows they like to moo (moo).
   Cows they like to moo (moo).
   Cows they like to moo (moo),
   Cows they like to moo (moo).
   Cows they like to moo (moo). Oh, yeah!

4. Wolves they like to howl (howl).
   Wolves they like to howl (howl).
   Wolves they like to howl (howl).
   Wolves they like to howl (howl).
   Wolves they like to howl (howl). Oh, yeah!

5. Cowboys like to cheer (yee-haw).
   Cowboys like to cheer (yee-haw).
   Cowboys like to cheer (yee-haw),
   Cowboys like to cheer (yee-haw).
   Cowboys like to cheer (yee-haw). Oh, yeah!

6. Cowboys like to go to sleep late at night (snore).
   Cowboys like to go to sleep late at night (snore).
   Cowboys like to sleep (snore),
   Cowboys like to sleep (snore).
   Late at night (snore). Oh, yeah!

If I Had a Fiddle

Pretending to play musical instruments is always lots of fun, and in this song children get to "play" instruments, sing about them, and make noises representing their sounds. Everyone will get to pretend to play a trumpet, a violin with the bow going across the strings, a piano with fingers wiggling as they move up and down the keyboard, and a banjo with one hand up on the imaginary fretboard and the other wiggling fingers like plucking the strings. Later you can add other instruments like a trombone, drums, or any others that the children can come up with.

Words and Music Adapted by
Ken Frawley

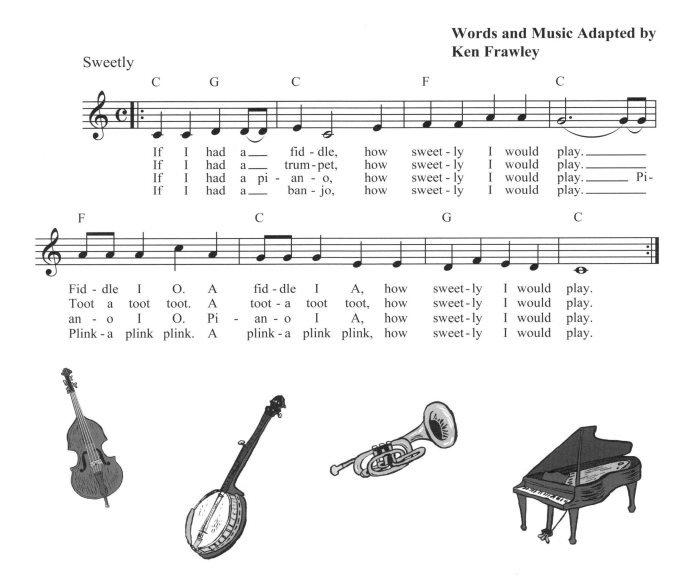

Sweetly

C   G   C   F   C

If I had a___ fid - dle, how sweet - ly I would play._____
If I had a___ trum - pet, how sweet - ly I would play._____
If I had a pi - an - o, how sweet - ly I would play._____ Pi-
If I had a___ ban - jo, how sweet - ly I would play._____

F   C   G   C

Fid - dle I O. A fid - dle I A, how sweet - ly I would play.
Toot a toot toot. A toot - a toot toot, how sweet - ly I would play.
an - o I O. Pi - an - o I A, how sweet - ly I would play.
Plink - a plink plink. A plink - a plink plink, how sweet - ly I would play.

Animal Choir

This is a great way to introduce children to the concept of singing different parts of a song all together as a choir. Children will first have the opportunity to sing sounds for all the animals, and then, as part of a group, they will get to focus on just their own individual animal sound. It is helpful to collect stuffed animals or pictures of animals that make sounds (cow, pig, lion, bird, wolf, etc.) and place them in a bag. One at a time, have children choose an animal, demonstrate the sound, and hold the animal up while everyone sings a verse featuring that animal's sound.

The song is broken into three parts. Part A is where all the animal sounds are introduced and everyone gets to sing. For part B, separate the children into groups led by a child holding an animal. Then have the children sing only their group's animal sound during their part to the song and remain quiet for the other animal sounds. At first, you'll find that it's helpful to break children into two groups; then, as the children become more familiar with the song, increase to three groups or more. Repeat this section a few times so that the children grasp the concept of singing only when it is their turn. Finally, for part C, each group will sing their animal sounds "all together now." All groups of children then make their animal sound at the same time. It can get a bit uproarious, and it's a great deal of fun! You can also add animal signs (many of which can be found in this book) to the song. Children then sing, sign, and make animal sounds.

Animal Choir

**Words and Music by
Ken Frawley**

Animal Choir

Up, Up, Up We Go!

This is a playful song about up and down. It has the children not only making the motions of pointing up and pointing down, but also singing in high and low voices. The song connects the concepts of up and high and down and low. Start the song with everyone sitting. As you sing "Up, up, up, up, up we go," everyone slowly stands up. Point fingers up on "singing high," and point fingers down on "singing low." Clap on the last line of the song. You can add other actions later that the children would like to do. It is a good song to move from active play to sitting activities as the song ends with everyone sitting down.

**Words and Music by
Georgia Frawley**

Stop, Look, and Listen

The movement in this song comes from the use of American Sign Language. Included are signs for key words used with young children: STOP, LOOK, and LISTEN. These signs are very useful at other times during the day. You can use them with children when crossing the street, walking through a parking lot, or playing in a park. The song also features signs for various modes of transportation including CAR, JET, and FIRE-TRUCK. Find this song on We Sign *Play Time*.

STOP - 1   STOP - 2   LOOK

LISTEN   YES/YEAH   TRAIN

CAR   FIRE-TRUCK
          (Shake hands)

Stop, Look, and Listen

Traditional Music Adapted
New Words by
Ken Frawley

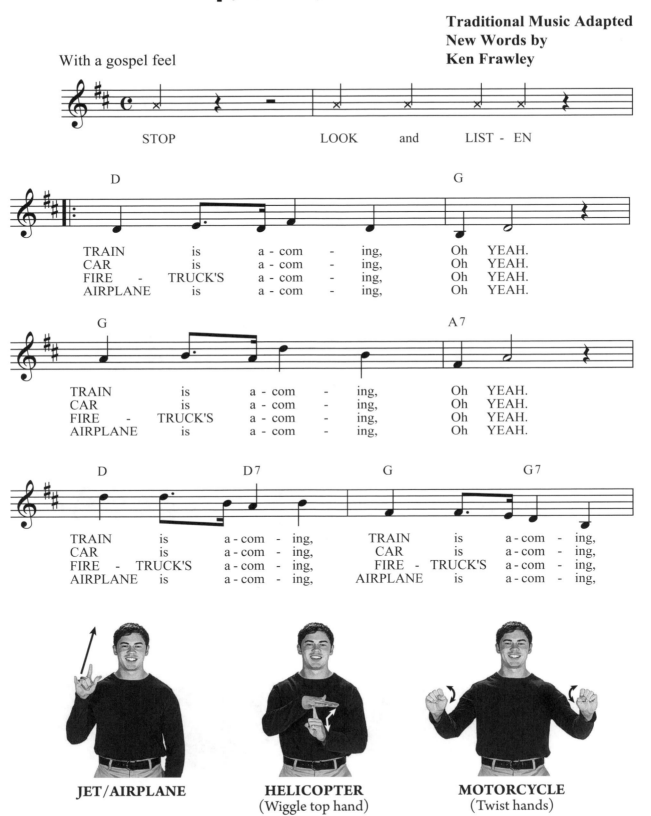

JET/AIRPLANE

HELICOPTER
(Wiggle top hand)

MOTORCYCLE
(Twist hands)

Stop, Look, and Listen

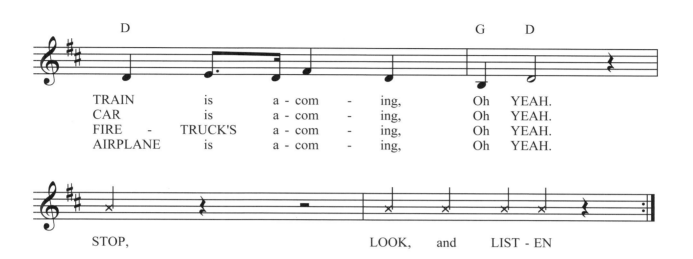

TRAIN is a - com - ing, Oh YEAH.
CAR is a - com - ing, Oh YEAH.
FIRE - TRUCK'S a - com - ing, Oh YEAH.
AIRPLANE is a - com - ing, Oh YEAH.

STOP, LOOK, and LIST - EN

5. HELICOPTER'S coming, oh YEAH.
HELICOPTER'S coming, oh YEAH.
HELICOPTER'S coming, helicopter's coming.
HELICOPTER'S coming, oh YEAH.
STOP, LOOK, and LISTEN.

6. MOTORCYCLE'S coming, oh YEAH.
MOTORCYCLE'S coming, oh YEAH.
MOTORCYCLE'S coming, motorcycle's coming.
MOTORCYCLE'S coming, oh YEAH.
STOP, LOOK, and LISTEN.

Walking Through the Forest

Take a walk through the forest in this song and look around for animals to imitate. Use your imagination—sing about any animal you wish, even if it does not actually live in the forest. Children just enjoy the engaged fun of this song. To add animals, you simply come up with an action each animal would do. I often have children choose the animal and then show me how that animal moves. Notice the tempo changes as the animal's movements change. Find the signed version of this song on We Sign *More Animals*.

Walking
(Act like walking)

Saw

Snake Slithering
(Slither)

Mother Duck Waddling
(Waddle)

Monkey Swinging
(Alternate arms & swing)

Kangaroo Hopping
(Hop)

Elephant Lumbering
(Swing arm like trunk)

Fish Swimming
(Hand acts like fish)

Eagle Soaring
(Imitate flying)

Walking Through the Forest

**Words and Music by
Ken Frawley**

Playfully

Walking Through the Forest

70

Walking Through the Forest

walked through the for-est this is what I saw: a mon-key swing-ing
branch to branch in a tall tree, an el-e-phant lum-
ber-ing by, oh— my! A kan-ga-roo
hop-ping with a ba-by in her pouch, a moth-er duck wad-dl-ing
with her fam-i-ly, and a snake slith-er-ing through tall grass,
yeah! And a snake slith-er-ing through tall grass.

6. As I walked through the forest, this is what I saw:
   An eagle soaring high up in the sky above me,
   A monkey swinging branch to branch in a tall tree,
   An elephant lumbering by, oh my!
   A kangaroo hopping with a baby in her pouch,
   A mother duck waddling with her family,
   And a snake slithering through tall grass, yeah!
   And a snake slithering through tall grass.

Dum Dum Dah Dah

Hand jives make songs interesting, challenging, and fun. With this song, teaching the melody while clapping hands and patting thighs slowly is best. Once the melody and beginning movements are established, slowly add the advanced movements to the song. Singing a cappella allows you to lead the movements for the children. Start out slowly and increase the tempo until you move and sing as fast as you can. The simple words in this song allow you to make up your own crazy, complicated, and silly movements as well. Have fun!

Beginning

Pat Thighs   **Clap Hands**

Advanced

R Flat Hands - 1   **L Flat Hands - 2**
(Move twice)   (Move twice)

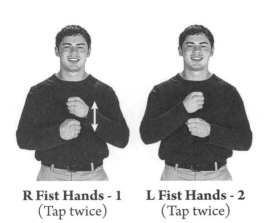

R Fist Hands - 1   **L Fist Hands - 2**
(Tap twice)   (Tap twice)

Roll Hands   **Hands Up High**

Dum Dum Dah Dah

Traditional

Slowly, then repeated with increasing tempo

	Dum,	dum,	dah, dah	dah	dum	dum	dah dah	dah
(Beginning) 1.	Pat	pat	clap	clap	pat	pat	clap	clap
(Advanced) 2.	Pat	pat	clap	clap	R flat	R flat	L flat	L flat

	dum	dum	dah dah dah	dum.	
1.	pat	pat	clap clap	pat pat	clap clap
2.	R fist	R fist	L fist L fist	roll hands /	hands up high

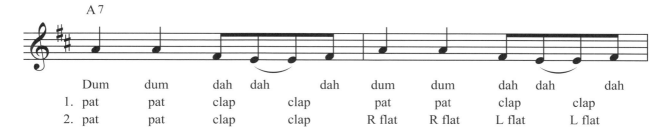

	Dum	dum	dah dah	dah	dum	dum	dah dah	dah
1.	pat	pat	clap	clap	pat	pat	clap	clap
2.	pat	pat	clap	clap	R flat	R flat	L flat	L flat

	dum	dum	dah dah dah	dum.	
1.	pat	pat	clap clap	pat pat	clap clap
2.	R fist	R fist	L fist L fist	roll hands /	hands up high

Can You Do?

Children use fine and gross motor skills while exercising their memories in this song. This is a "zipper" song—it gets longer and longer with each verse. Once you have learned the song as written, have the children choose their own actions. Have a few actions ready to suggest when children are not sure about what to do (e.g. laughing, making silly faces, looking up, smiling, or patting your head and rubbing your stomach). You can control the level of activity by having the children choose actions like jumping or hopping when they can stand and move around and wiggling, waving, or making animal sounds when sitting is required.

Music and Lyrics by
Ken Frawley Amanda Carnegie

Can You Do?

G7

1. C 3 C7

nose? (touch nose) Can you fol-low a-long with me? Can you
hands? (clap, clap) Can you
around? (wiggle) Can you

F D7 C G7 C

do the things you see? Can you touch your nose? Can you

2. C C7 F D7 C G7

clap your hands? Can you touch your nose? Can you do the things I

C 3. C C7 F D7

do? Can you wiggle all around? Can you clap your hands? Can you

C G7 C

touch your nose? Can you do the things I do?

4. Can you wink your eyes?
   Can you wink your eyes?
   Can you wink your eyes?
   Can you wiggle all around?
   Can you clap your hands?
   Can you touch your nose?
   Can you do the things I do?

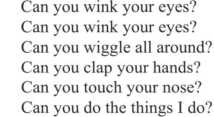

My Hands by My Side

This great old folk song deals with body parts in a fun and silly way. Children will simply point to the related body part when singing about that part. Once you have learned the song, you can add your own silly verses featuring body parts like mouth talker, chin chomper, bread basket (stomach), and knee knocker. Begin each verse with your hands by your side, moving them in an arching movement for the words "my hands" and back to standing at attention for "by my side." You will end each verse with the silly actions for "inky dinky do" and finally clap for the last line. This is a "zipper" song—it keeps getting longer and longer as each new verse is added, making the song more and more challenging.

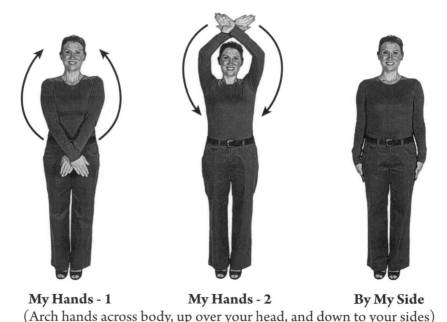

My Hands - 1   **My Hands - 2**   **By My Side**
(Arch hands across body, up over your head, and down to your sides)

Inky Dinky   **Do**

My Hands by My Side

Traditional

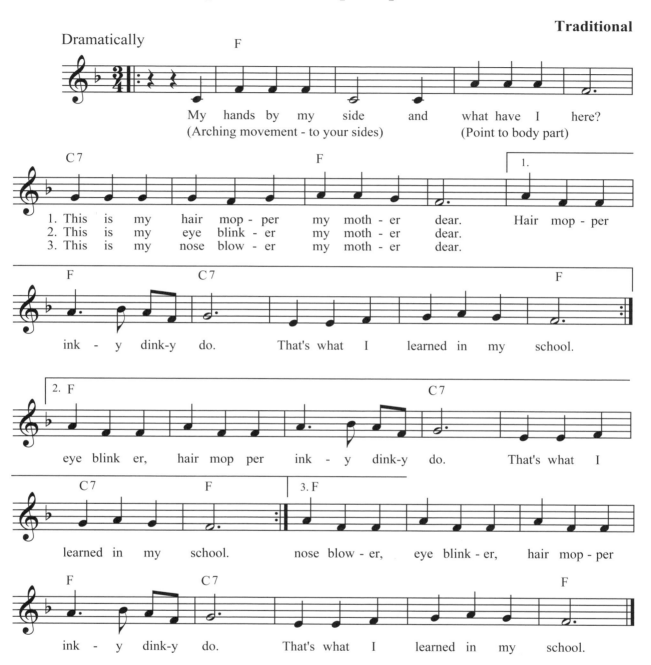

My hands by my side and what have I here?
(Arching movement - to your sides)   (Point to body part)

1. This is my hair mop-per my moth-er dear. Hair mop-per
2. This is my eye blink-er my moth-er dear.
3. This is my nose blow-er my moth-er dear.

ink - y dink-y do. That's what I learned in my school.

eye blink er, hair mop per ink - y dink-y do. That's what I

learned in my school. nose blow - er, eye blink - er, hair mop-per

ink - y dink-y do. That's what I learned in my school.

Other Suggestions

4. Hand clappers
5. Toe tappers

Mouth talker	Bread basket
Chin chomper	Waist twister
Shoulder shrugger	Hip swinger
Elbow bender	Knee knockers

Transposition Chart

You may find that the notes you are singing are too high or too low for your children. This transposition chart will allow you to easily change a song's key. Follow these four steps:

1. Determine the key. Look up the first chord in the first full measure of the song. (It is the same as the chord in the last measure of the song.) This is the key. For example, if you find that the first and last chord in a song is D – the song is in the key of D.

2. Look at the key's "family of chords." Look to the Key column for D on the chart below. The chords in the "family of D" are found by moving across the chart, from left to right, through the major, minor, and additional columns. The chords in the D family are: G major, A major, F# minor, B minor, and E seventh major.

3. Raising and lowering a key. To lower a key you move up the chart. (Once you reach the top, begin again at the bottom.) To raise a key and make it higher, you move down the chart. (Once you reach the bottom, begin again at the top.)

4. Change a key. To lower a song in the key of D, just a little, you would move to the bottom of the chart to the key of C. You would then change all chords in the "family of D" to the corresponding chords in the new "family of C." For example, look to the song *Cowboys Like to Ride* (page 59). It is in the key of D and the "family of D" includes D, A⁷, and G. To change this song to the key of C you would replace all D chords with C, all A⁷ chords with G⁷, and all G chords with F. To raise this same song up, just a little, you would change all the D chords with the "family of E" chords. All D chords would become E, all A⁷ chords would become B⁷, and all G chords would become A.

5. Play the song in the new key. You are now ready to play and sing this song in the key of C or E. Follow these basic steps to change any song into a new higher or lower key.

Key	Major 4th	Major 5th	Minor	Minor	Additional
D	G	A	F#m	Bm	E7
E	A	B	G#m	C#m	F#7
F	Bb	C	Am	Dm	G7
G	C	D	Bm	Em	A7
A	D	E	C#m	F#m	B7
B	E	F#	D#m	G#m	C#7
C	F	G	Em	Am	C7

NOTE: This transposition chart is for use with *Play-Along Songs* and reflects the chords used in our music collections.

Contributing Artists

Ken Frawley – Ken has been writing, recording, and performing interactive play-along songs with children for over 30 years. He performs regularly at schools, libraries, preschools, and other events throughout Southern California and has presented his music to over 1 million children and families. He co-produced the We Sign DVD series that has won over 50 national awards of excellence, and co-wrote the Sign to Speak series of books designed to teach parents, teachers, early childhood professionals, and caregivers how to use American Sign Language effectively with children at various stages of development. Ken has lectured and presented workshops across the country on using playful and interactive songs in education and just for fun. Currently he has a variety of albums and hundreds of songs available on iTunes. Visit www.production-associates.com, look under music and you can link to iTunes to listen to and download songs. Contact Ken at info@playalongsongs.com.

Georgia Frawley, MA – Georgia has taught Child Development, Marriage and Family, Parenting, Physical Education and Careers with Children for over 30 years. As part of her curriculum, she regularly included participatory play-along songs as a means to teach her students how to play, interact, and communicate with children. She has performed at library and city events for over 25 years, co-produced the We Sign DVD series, and co-wrote the Sign to Speak books. Contact Georgia at info@playalongsongs.com.

Resources For Home and School

~ DVDs ~
We Sign

Babies & Toddlers 2—Signing DVD that features top signs, easy-to-follow instructions, tips, and insights. Over 200 words and baby songs included.

Baby Songs—Features songs to sign to your baby including "Mary Had a Little Lamb," "Hush Little Baby," "How Many Legs?," and more.

Play Time—Interactive songs that include "The Wheels on the Bus," "One Little Kitty," "If You're Happy," "Stop, Look, and Listen," and more.

Fun Time—Playful songs that include "Old MacDonald," "Little Miss Muffet," "A Little Song in My Heart," "Row, Row, Row Your Boat," and more.

ABC—Learn ABCs, first letter sounds, and finger spelling with "The ABC Song," "ABC Object Song," and "S M I L E."

Numbers—Discover numbers one to one hundred with songs that include "One, Two, Buckle My Shoe," "One Little Bird," "Ten to One Hundred," and more.

Colors—Learn all about colors with songs like "The Color Song," "Mixing All My Colors," "The Snowman's Hat," and more.

Rhymes—Sign and sing along to Mother Goose rhymes like "Mary Had a Little Lamb," "Twinkle, Twinkle, Little Star," "Humpty Dumpty," and many more.

Animals—A fun way to learn and remember animals. Songs include "Itsy Bitsy Spider," "The Bear Went Over the Mountain," "Animals of the Alphabet," and more.

Classroom Favorites—Signing songs to use all year round including "Earth, Earth, Earth," "Jingle Bells," "Bingo," "Home on the Range," and more.

More Animals—Learn about animals and habitats with songs like "Animals Live All Around the World," "They Call Home," "Walking Through the Forest," and more.

Patriotic Songs—Songs included are "Yankee Doodle," "America," "Battle Hymn of the Republic," "The Star-Spangled Banner," and more.

Christmas Carols—Wonderful hymns and carols to sing with signs including "Silent Night," "Joy to the World," "O Little Town of Bethlehem," and more.

Santa's Favorite Christmas Songs—Features "O Christmas Tree," "Up on the House Top," "The Twelve Days of Christmas," "We Wish You a Merry Christmas," and more.

WESIGN.COM

~ Books ~
Sign To Speak

Babies Can Talk—Comprehensive program to learn how to sign successfully with babies. Includes effective signs, clear pictures, tips, insights, and activities.

Toddlers at Play—A program for parents, teachers, and caregivers to use sign language successfully with toddlers. Includes effective signs, clear pictures, tips, insights, songs, games, and more.

SIGNTOSPEAK.COM

Play Along Songs

Play-Along Songs, Volume 1—The first book in our series of playful interactive songs for children of all ages.

Play-Along Songs, Volume 2—More songs featuring movement, language use, and ASL. Fun and playful for all ages.

PLAYALONGSONGS.COM